THE BOOK OF
POSITIVE
THOUGHTS

A Helen Exley
QUOTATION COLLECTION

Helen Exley

ILLUSTRATED BY JULIETTE CLARKE
EDITED BY HELEN EXLEY
Published in 2018 by Helen Exley®LONDON in Great Britain
Illustrated by Juliette Clarke©Helen Exley Creative Ltd 2018
Design and creation by Helen Exley©Helen Exley Creative
Ltd 2018. All the words by Pam Brown, Pamela Dugdale,
Stuart&Linda Macfarlane are © Helen Exley
Creative Ltd 2018.

ISBN 978-1-78485-145-3
12 11 10 9 8 7 6 5 4 3 2 1

OTHER BOOKS IN THE SERIES
LIVE! LOVE! LAUGH!   BELIEVE in YOURSELF   FOREVER TOGETHER
CALM AND MINDFULNESS   THE RESILIENCE BOOK

Helen Exley®LONDON, 16 Chalk Hill,
Watford, Hertfordshire, WD19 4BG, UK.
www.helenexley.com

THE BOOK OF
POSITIVE
THOUGHTS

A Helen Exley
QUOTATION COLLECTION

The moment when you first wake up in the morning is the most wonderful of the twenty-four hours. No matter how weary or dreary you may feel, you possess the certainty that, during the day that lies before you, absolutely anything may happen. And the fact that it practically always doesn't, matters not a jot. The possibility is always there.

MONICA BALDWIN

Every day brings a chance for you to draw in a breath, kick off your shoes, and dance.

OPRAH WINFREY, B. 1954

Opportunity dances with those who are already on the dance floor.

H. JACKSON BROWN JR. B. 1940

Life is a great big canvas; throw all the paint on it you can.

DANNY KAYE (1913 - 1987)

The most revolutionary act
one can commit in our world
is to be happy.

HUNTER "PATCH" ADAMS, B. 1945

Your life
is an occasion.
Rise to it.

SUZANNE WEYN, B. 1955

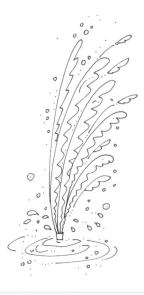

*In the depth of winter,
I finally learned
that within me
there lay an invincible
summer.*

ALBERT CAMUS (1913 - 1960)

It is confidence in our bodies, minds, and spirits that allows us to keep looking for new adventures, new directions to grow in, and new lessons to learn – which is what life is all about.

OPRAH WINFREY, B. 1954

Every day is a birth day; every moment of it is new to us; we are born again, renewed for fresh work and endeavour.

ISAAC WATTS (1674 - 1748)

If you hear a voice within you say "You are not a painter," then by all means paint, and that voice will be silenced.

VINCENT VAN GOGH (1853 - 1890)

Our actions, which are driven by our feelings, offer us the opportunity to live; they let us go out and leave a mark… Actions cause things to happen and from those outcomes we learn, we improve and we find the best path for an amazing existence. We make our own masterpiece. And it all starts from a blank canvas.

JONNY WILKINSON, B. 1979

*The positive thinker
sees the invisible,
feels the intangible,
and achieves
the impossible.*

SIR WINSTON CHURCHILL (1874 - 1965)

We should be blessed if we lived in the present always, and took advantage of every accident that befell us, like the grass which confesses the influence of the slightest dew that falls on it; and did not spend our time in atoning for the neglect of past opportunities… We loiter in winter while it is already spring.

HENRY DAVID THOREAU (1817 - 1862)

Today is the first da

It does not matter how long you are spending on the earth, how much money you have gathered or how much attention you have received. It is the amount of positive vibration you have radiated in life that matters.

AMIT RAY

f the rest of your life.

DALE CARNEGIE (1888 - 1955)

What would you attempt to do if you knew you could not fail?

DR. ROBERT SCHULLER (1926- 2015)

*Y*es is the most powerful word.
Yes is freeing and inspiring.
It means permission.
It means possibility.
It means you give yourself
and others the chance to dream.
Saying yes
makes you feel good.

HOWARD BEHAR, B. 1944

I wish I knew what people meant when they say they find "emptiness" in this wonderful adventure of living, which seems to me to pile up its glories like an horizon-wide sunset as the light declines. I'm afraid I'm an incorrigible life-lover, life-wanderer, and adventurer.

EDITH WHARTON (1862 - 1937)

Express yourself completely, then keep quiet.
Be like the forces of nature:
When it blows, there is only wind;
When it rains, there is only rain;
When the clouds pass, the sun shines through.

LAO TZU (604 B.C. - 531 B.C.)

... if we say, "It's absolutely freezing today! I'll probably catch a cold before the end of the day!" then our words expose a negative attitude. But if we say, "The temperature is very cold" (a simple statement of fact), then our expressions, and therefore attitude, are not negative. Sustaining an alert state in which self-awareness becomes possible gives us a chance to discover the origins of negativity. In doing so, we also have an opportunity to arrive at a state of positiveness, so that our words and deeds are also positive, making others feel comfortable, cheerful, and inspired.

H.E. DAVEY, B. 1961

*Hundreds of flowers
in spring, the moon
in autumn, a cool breeze
in summer, and snow
in winter. If there is no
vain cloud in your mind,
for you every day
is a good day.*

WU MEN

If we remain pessimistic, thinking that we cannot succeed, then we aren't able to evolve. The thought that we cannot compete with others is the first step toward failure.

THE DALAI LAMA, B. 1935

Whatever in you is negative or dark,
fight it, get it out, put the light on it,
and turn it around and make it positive.

FRANCES LEAR

At the end of a difficult day, congratulate yourself on your achievements no matter how small they may seem. Celebrate your life. Tomorrow is another day in that life and you deserve it to be a happy and successful day.

STUART & LINDA MACFARLANE

Anyone who masters the grey everyday is a hero.

FYODOR MIKHAILOVICH DOSTOYEVSKY (1821 - 1881)

Life is fun

Life is happiness

Life is gladness

Life is loving

Life is helping

Life is gentleness

Life is laughter

Oh life is beautiful.

ALLISON HUDDART, AGE 10

Every day I wake up, I think, what a blessing – I'm alive. I don't care if it snows, it rains, it thunderstorms – a heatwave. I think, I'm here – this is terrific.

RICHARD HARRIS (1930 - 2002)

Life is like a blanket, too short. You pull it up and your toes rebel, you yank it down and shivers meander about your shoulder; but cheerful folks manage to draw their knees up and pass a very comfortable night.

MARION HOWARD

*W*hen your house
has quite disappeared,
you mustn't complain.
You still have
all that snow to do with
what you like.

FROM "EEYORE'S GLOOMY LITTLE INSTRUCTION BOOK"

To improve the golden moment of
opportunity, and catch the good that is
within our reach, is the great art of life.

DR. SAMUEL JOHNSON (1709 - 1784)

Whatever you attempt, go at it with spirit.
Put some in!

DAVID STARR JORDAN (1851 - 1931)

If we had keen vision
of all that is ordinary
in human life,
it would be like hearing
the grass grow or
the squirrel's heartbeat,
and we should die
of that roar
which is the other side
of silence.

GEORGE ELIOT (MARY ANN EVANS) (1819 - 1880)

If I were to wish for anything, I should not wish for wealth and power, but for the passionate sense of the potential. For the eye which, ever young and ardent, sees the possible… what wine is so sparkling, so fragrant, so intoxicating, as possibility!

SØREN KIERKEGAARD (1813 - 1855)

Whether you think you can or you can't, you're right!

HENRY FORD (1863 - 1947)

Fall seven times

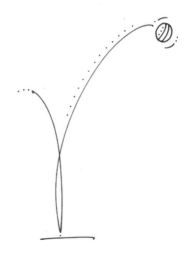

Stand up eight.

JAPANESE PROVERB

Few things in the world are more powerful than a positive push. A smile. A word of optimism and hope. A "you can do it" when things are tough.

RICHARD M. DEVOS, B. 1926

You will do foolish things but do them with enthusiasm.

SIDONIE GABRIELLE COLETTE (1873 - 1954)

Seven keys to getting more things done:

1. Start
2. Don't make excuses
3. Celebrate small steps
4. Ignore critics
5. Be consistent
6. Be open
7. Stay positive

GERMANY KENT, B. 1975

There is an excitement in challenge,
in daring to fling open doors
– and if it all fails
it is not loss but learning.

PAM BROWN (1928 - 2014)

In every day,
there are 1,440 minutes.
That means we have 1,440
daily opportunities
to make a positive impact.

LES BROWN

Hope is a waking

*Give every day
the chance to become
the most beautiful
of your life.*

MARK TWAIN (1835 - 1910)

ream. ARISTOTLE (384 B.C. - 322 B.C)

*When you arise
in the morning think of
what a privilege it is
to be alive, to think,
to enjoy, to love...*

MARCUS AURELIUS (A.D. 121 - 180)

I live by one principle: Enjoy life with no conditions! People say, "If I had your health, if I had your money, oh, I would enjoy myself." It is not true. I would be happy if I were lying sick in a hospital bed. It must come from the inside. That is the one thing I hope to have contributed to my children, by example and by talk: to make no conditions, to understand that life is a wonderful thing and to enjoy it, every day, to the full.

ARTHUR RUBINSTEIN (1887 - 1982)

I shall no longer allow negative thoughts or
feelings to drain me of my energy. Instead
I shall focus on all the good that is in my life.
I will think it, feel it and speak it. By doing so
I will send out vibes of positive energy into
the world and I shall be grateful for all the
wonderful things it will attract into my life.

AUTHOR UNKNOWN

Isn't that the most fabulous thing about life?
Keep your mind open and the universe
will just come in and give you presents
the entire time.

STEPHANIE BEACHAM, B. 1947

Faint not –
fight on!
Tomorrow
comes the song.

MALTBIE BABCOCK (1858 - 1901)

There are two ways of spreading light:
to be the candle or the mirror that reflects.

EDITH WHARTON (1862 - 1937)

I have a lot of things
to prove to myself.
One is that I can live
my life fearlessly.

OPRAH WINFREY, B. 1954

I would be true,
for there are those who trust me;
I would be pure,
for there are those who care;
I would be strong,
for there is much to suffer;
I would be brave,
for there is much to dare.
I would be friend of all –
the foe, the friendless;
I would be giving
and forget the gift;
I would be humble,
for I know my weakness;
I would look up –
and laugh – and love – and lift.

HOWARD ARNOLD WALTER (1883 – 1918)

I would
look
up...

I don't want to get to the end of my life and find that I just lived the length of it. I want to have lived the width of it as well.

DIANE ACKERMAN, B. 1948

Increase your happy times, letting yourself go; follow your desire and best advantage. And "do your thing" while you are still on this earth, according to the command of your heart.

AFRICAN PROVERB

*Enthusiasm is the yeast
that makes your hopes rise
to the stars.
Enthusiasm is the sparkle
in your eyes, the swing
in your gait,
the grip of your hand,
the irresistible surge of will
and energy to excite
your ideas.*

HENRY TOR

You've got to be energetic. You've got to have
a passion which comes from every tentacle
of your body, and you've got to make that
passion a reality.

ANITA RODDICK (1942 - 2007)

*T*he future belongs
to those who believe
in the beauty
of their dreams.

ELEANOR ROOSEVELT (1884 - 1962)

*You see things;
and you say, "Why?"
But I dream things
that never were and I say,
"Why not?"*

GEORGE BERNARD SHAW (1856 - 1950)

Do not put off till tomorrow
what can be enjoyed today.

JOSH BILLINGS (1818 - 1885)

Life engenders life.
Energy creates energy.
It is by spending oneself
that one becomes rich.

SARAH BERNHARDT (1844 - 1923)

There are two paths through life; one is a tortuous uphill struggle over rocky terrain squeezing through thorny briars; the other leads you across grassy dales with fragrant flowers past beautiful lochs with breathtaking mountains beyond. The paths are the same – attitude of mind makes them seem different.

STUART & LINDA MACFARLANE

You've done it before and you can do it now. See the positive possibilities. Redirect the substantial energy of your frustration and turn it into positive, effective, unstoppable determination.

RALPH MARSTON

We can complain because rose bushes have thorns, or rejoice because thorn bushes have roses.

ABRAHAM LINCOLN (1809 - 1865)

Successful people maintain a positive focus in life no matter what is going on around them. They stay focused on their past successes rather than their past failures, and on the next action steps they need to take to get them closer to the fulfilment of their goals rather than all the other distractions that life presents to them.

JACK CANFIELD

I like living. I have sometimes been wildly, despairingly, acutely miserable, racked with sorrow, but through it all I still know quite certainly that just to be alive is a grand thing.

AGATHA CHRISTIE (1890 - 1976)

*N*othing is quite
as thrilling as the voyage
from darkness to light,
from "I can't" to "I can".

...we are all waves of the same ocean. Some days the wave is big, some days it is small. Surf the wave you are given today and experience the rolling heights it offers. Validate yourself, your abilities, your gifts, your understandings. Validate your uniqueness...

Like a salmon swimming upstream, internal resistance challenges us to move against our fears and doubts. You can experience the same challenges with a positive focus or a negative focus. Find the positive and build on that. It will snowball into greater celebration.

BLACKWOLF (ROBERT JONES), OJIBWE, AND GINA JONES

Laughing cheerfulness
throws sunlight
on all the paths of life.

JEAN PAUL RICHTER (1763 - 1825)

No matter how negative my day turns out, there is always one positive treasure to be found: a beautiful sunset, a baby's smile, the soothing songs of the birds! Nothing extraordinary, but how it helps us to see: *la vie en rose.*

INGE BRANDT

Even after a bad harvest there must be a sowing.

SENECA THE YOUNGER (4 B.C. - A.D. 65)

When one door shu

Never look back unless you are planning to go that way.

HENRY DAVID THOREAU (1817 - 1862)

nother opens.

SAMUEL PALMER (1805 - 1881)

A positive thinker does not refuse to recognize the negative, he refuses to dwell on it. Positive thinking is a form of thought which habitually looks for the best results from the worst conditions.

NORMAN VINCENT PEALE (1898 - 1993)

No pessimist ever discovered the secrets of the stars, or sailed to an uncharted land, or opened a new heaven to the human spirit.

HELEN KELLER
(BORN BOTH DEAF AND BLIND) (1880 - 1968)

Don't think about what might go wrong,

think about what could go right.

Forget the mistake.

Remember the lesson.

AUTHOR UNKNOWN

You may not control all the events that happen to you, but you can decide not to be reduced by them. Do not complain. Make every effort to change things you do not like. If you cannot make a change, change the way you have been thinking. You might find a new solution.

MAYA ANGELOU (1928 - 2014)

REASONS TO CELEBRATE

A day off work.
A birthday.
A non-birthday!
The first snow.
The first snowdrops.
Seeing a new baby.
Finishing writing that poem.
Buying a new outfit.
A trip to the park.

STUART & LINDA MACFARLANE

When unhappiness
overwhelms you,
when you end up
wishing for an eternal night
to fall on the world,
think of the greenery which
springs up after the rain,
think of the awakening
of a child.

AMIN MAALOUF, B. 1949

*E*ach day has a rarity…
*I could put it in a vase
and admire it,
like the first dandelions…*

MARGARET LAWRENCE (1896 - 1973)

No more brooding,

No more despondency.

Your life will become

The beauty of a rose,

The song of the dawn,

The dance of twilight.

SRI CHINMOY (1931 - 2007)

I still find each day too short for all the
thoughts I want to think, all the walks I want
to take, all the books I want to read, and all
the friends I want to see.

JOHN BURROUGHS (1837 - 1921)

*The weather forecast says
"Rain! Rain! Rain!"
but your heart says
"Sun! Sun! Sun!"*

STUART & LINDA MACFARLANE

To be able to look backwards and say,
"This, this, has been the finest year of my life,"
that is glorious!
But anticipation. To be able to look ahead
and say, "The next year can and shall be
better," that is more glorious!

FRANK LAUBACH (1884 - 1970)

Far away there in the sunshine are my highest aspirations. I may not reach them, but I can look up and see their beauty, believe in them, and try to follow where they lead.

LOUISA MAY ALCOTT (1832 - 1888)

You are the sum total of everything you've ever seen, heard, eaten, smelled, been told, forgot – it's all there. Everything influences each of us, and because of that I try to make sure that my experiences are positive.

MAYA ANGELOU (1928 - 2014)

Don't put a ceilin

Positive thoughts generate
positive feelings and attract
positive life experiences.
One small positive thought
in the morning can change
the entire outcome of your day.

AUTHOR UNKNOWN

n yourself.

OPRAH WINFREY, B. 1954

*I go everywhere
without hesitation.
Hallelujah!*

VIRGINIA BRINDIS DE SALAS

*You have to trust
in something –
your gut, destiny, life,
karma, whatever…
it has made
all the difference
in my life.*

The differe

I'm a very positive thinker,
and I think that
is what helps me the most
in difficult moments.

ROGER FEDERER, B. 1981

*Y*ou can transcend all
negativity when you realize
that the only power it has
over you is your belief in it.
As you experience this truth
about yourself
you are set free.

EILEEN CADDY (1917 - 2006)

I think that you must try. You have to try to be nice, try to be positive, try to make a go of things. Try to make a party a good one, try to say thank you for everything you've got and be grateful to people. Don't just sit back and expect things to happen.

JOANNA LUMLEY, B. 1946

If *you ask me*
what I came
into this life
to do,
I will tell you:
I came to live
out loud.

EMILE ZOLA (1840 - 1902)

Let us go singing
as far as we go:
the road
will be less tedious.

VIRGIL (70 B.C. - 19 B.C.)

Be content

with what you have;

rejoice in the way things are.

When you realise

there is nothing lacking,

the whole world

belongs to you.

LAO TZU (604 B.C. - 531 B.C.)

A new life begins for us with every second. Let us go forward joyously to meet it. We must press on, whether we will or no, and we shall walk better with our eyes before us than with them ever cast behind.

JEROME K. JEROME (1859 - 1927)

Write the bad things that are done to you in sand, but write the good things that happen to you on a piece of marble.

ARAB PROVERB

When you are joyful, when you say yes to life and have fun and project positivity all around you, you become a sun in the centre of every constellation, and people want to be near you.

SHANNON L. ALDER

Joyful!

One day most of the family was together in the mailroom, busily sorting through stacks of letters.
Will was on the floor playing.
He looked up and said,
"Mommy, Daddy can't move his arms anymore."
Dana said, "That's right, Daddy can't move his arms."
"And Daddy can't run around anymore."

"That's right; he can't run around anymore."

"And Daddy can't talk."

"That's right; he can't talk right now, but he will be able to."

Then Will paused, screwed up his face in concentration, and burst out happily, "But he can still smile." Everyone put down what they were doing and just looked at one another.

CHRISTOPHER REEVE (1952 - 2004)

When life gives a hundred reasons to break down and cry, show life that you have a thousand reasons to smile and laugh. Stay Strong.

AUTHOR UNKNOWN

*Though no one
can go back and make
a brand new start,
anyone can start now
and make
a brand new ending.*

CARL BARD

*The longer I live,
the more apparent
it becomes to me
that paradise is not
a goal at the end
of the road,
but the road itself.*

DOLLY PARTON, B. 1946

An entire water of the sea can't sink a ship unless it gets inside the ship. Similarly, negativity of the world can't put you down unless you allow it to get inside you.

GOI NASU

Cultivate an optimistic mind,
use your imagination,
always consider alternatives,
and dare to believe
that you can make possible
what others think is impossible.

RODOLFO COSTA

It takes but one positive thought
when given a chance to survive
and thrive to overpower
an entire army
of negative thoughts.

DR. ROBERT SCHULLER (1926 - 2015)

You *have your brush,*
you have your colours,
you paint paradise,
then in you go.

NIKOS KAZANTZAKIS (1883 - 1957)

I have always been delighted at the prospect of a new day, a fresh try, one more start, with perhaps a bit of magic waiting somewhere behind the morning.

J. B. PRIESTLEY (1894 - 1984)

Happiness, not in another place but this place... not for another hour, but this hour.

WALT WHITMAN (1819 - 1892)

Nothing i.

This is the best day the world has ever seen. Tomorrow will be better.

R. A. CAMPBELL

Nothing is impossible
Throw back the shoulders,
let the heart sing,
let the eyes flash,
let the mind be lifted up,
look upward and say to yourself...
nothing is impossible.

NORMAN VINCENT PEALE (1898 - 1993)

Ecstasy is full, deep involvement in life.

JOHN LOVELL

Never lose an opportunity
of seeing anything that is beautiful…
Welcome beauty in every fair face,
in every fair sky, in every flower…

RALPH WALDO EMERSON (1803 - 1882)

If we did
all the things
we are capable
of doing,
we would
literally
astound
ourselves.

THOMAS EDISON (1847 - 1931)

*F*ear less, hope more;
eat less, chew more;
whine less, breathe more;
talk less, say more;
love more,
and all good things
will be yours.

SWEDISH PROVERB

Be soft. Do not let the world make you hard. Do not let pain make you hate. Do not let the bitterness steal your sweetness. Take pride that even though the rest of the world may disagree, you still believe it to be a beautiful place.

KURT VONNEGUT (1922 - 2007)

Never run ou

f goals.

EARL NIGHTINGALE (1921 - 1989)

While you're going through the process of trying to find the satisfaction in your work, pretend you feel satisfied. Tell yourself you had a good day. Walk through the corridors with a smile rather than a scowl. Your positive energy will radiate. If you act like you're having fun, you'll find you are having fun.

JEAN CHATZKY, B. 1964

Let your body tell you you're powerful and deserving, and you become more present, enthusiastic and authentically yourself.

AMY CUDDY, B. 1972

I have a sort of enthusiasm for life and I don't ever want to lose it. I like my life. I like who I am and what I do and I'm quite at peace with myself.

JOAN COLLINS, B. 1933

*The biggest quality
in successful people,
I think, is an impatience
with negative thinking...
my feeling was, even if
it's as bad as I think it is,
we'll make it work.*

EDWARD MCCABE

To awaken each morning with a smile brightening my face; to greet the day with reverence for the opportunities it contains; to approach my work with a clean mind; to hold ever before me, even in the doing of little things, the ultimate purpose toward which I am working; to meet men and women with laughter on my lips and love in my heart; to be gentle, kind, and courteous through all the hours; to approach the night with weariness that ever woos sleep and the joy that comes from work well done – this is how I desire to waste wisely my days.

THOMAS DEKKER (c.1570 - 1632)

Positivity is a magn

r success.

STUART & LINDA MACFARLANE

I want to live for ecstasy. Small doses, moderate loves, all half-shades, leave me cold. I like extravagance. Letters which give the postman a stiff back to carry, books which overflow from their covers, sexuality which bursts the thermometers.

ANAÏS NIN (1903 - 1977)

Ecst

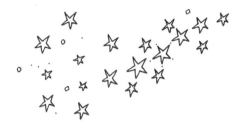

It seems to me that we can never give up longing and wishing while we are thoroughly alive. There are certain things we feel to be beautiful and good, and we must hunger after them.

GEORGE ELIOT (MARY ANN EVANS) (1819 - 1880)

*Two men looked out of
the prison bars;
The one saw mud;
the other saw stars.*

FREDERICK LANGBRIDGE (1849 - 1923)

Like the weather,
life is essentially variable…
and a healthy person believes
in the validity of his high hours
even when he is having
a low one.

HARRY EMERSON FOSDICK (1878 - 1969)

*Every problem
has a gift for you
in its hands.*

RICHARD BACH, B. 1936

It's often possible to turn negative situations into positive. Never feel a situation is all negative. There's a counterpart that is positive. Look for it, reach for it, utilize it – it will offset the negative.

BEAR HEART (MUSKOGEE) (1918 - 2008)

Your thoughts create your feelings. To save yourself from useless and painful feelings, don't think about useless or negative things.

DADI JANKI, B. 1916

Saying yes means getting up and acting on your belief that you can create meaning and purpose in whatever life hands you.

SUSAN JEFFERS (1938 - 2012)

*A*ll theory is grey,
but the golden tree of life
grows green.

JOHANN WOLFGANG VON GOETHE (1749 - 1832)

Your thoughts and your words define your life. Think positively and affirm positive words to enrich your life positively.

LAILAH GIFTY AKITA

You can't use up creativity. The more you use, the more you have.

MAYA ANGELOU (1928 - 2014)

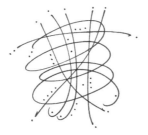

To say yes,
you have to sweat
and roll up
your sleeves
and plunge
both hands into life
up to the elbows.

JEAN ANOUILH (1910 - 1987)

In the morning, how good it is to see the brilliant light of the blessed summer day, always brightest just after rain, and to see how every tree and plant is full of new life and abounding gladness; and to feel one's own thankfulness of heart, and that it is good to live...

GERTRUDE JEKYLL (1843 - 1932)

Your plan for work and happiness should be big, imaginative and daring. Strike out boldly for the things you honestly want more than anything else in the world. The mistake is to put your sights too low, not to raise them too high.

HENRY J. KAISER

I avoid looking forward or backward, and try to keep looking upward.

CHARLOTTE BRONTË (1816 - 1855)

*Nothing great
was ever achieved
without enthusiasm.
The way of life
is wonderful;
it is by abandonment.*

RALPH WALDO EMERSON (1803 - 1882)

You must learn day by day, year by year,
to broaden your horizon. The more things you
love, the more you are interested in, the more
you enjoy, the more you are indignant about –
the more you have left when anything happen

ETHEL BARRYMORE (1879 - 1959)

It's not about winning or losing, it is about having the opportunity to be in it, to really live your life, to have purpose, and to enjoy it.

BILLIE JEAN KING, B. 1943

Work hard for what you want because it won't come to you without a fight. You have to be strong and courageous and know that you can do anything you put your mind to. If somebody puts you down or criticizes you, just keep on believing in yourself and turn it into something positive.

LEAH LABELLE

What is alive, and open, and active, is good. All that makes for inertia, lifelessness, dreariness, is bad.

D. H. LAWRENCE (1885 - 1930)

*E*veryone,
every single human being
in the world,
has something to give.
Something good.
Something wonderful.

PAM BROWN (1928 - 2014)

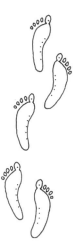

***K**eep*
a green tree
in your heart
and perhaps
a singing bird
will come.

CHINESE PROVERB

You're going to go through
tough times – that's life.
But I say,
"Nothing happens to you,
it happens for you."
See the positive in negative events.

JOEL OSTEEN, B. 1963

If there has been a secret
to my success –
a key ingredient or
a personal philosophy –
it is don't take no
for an answer
when you must hear yes.

JUNE JACKSON CHRISTMAS

Nothing has to happen for me to feel good!
I feel good because I'm alive! Life is a gift,
and I revel in it.

ANTHONY ROBBINS

There is in us an upwelling spring of life, energy, love, whatever you like to call it. If a course is not cut for it, it turns the ground round it to swamp.

MARK RUTHERFORD (1831 - 1913)

*W*rite it on your heart
that every day is
the best day of the year.

RALPH WALDO EMERSON (1803 - 1882)

My heart is fixed firm and stable in the belief
that ultimately the sunshine and the Summer,
the flowers and the azure sky, shall become as
it were, interwoven into our existence; we shall
take from all their beauty and enjoy their glory

RICHARD JEFFERIES (1848 - 1887)

Success is getting what you want and happiness
is wanting what you get.

IBO PROVERB

The main thing is having a positive approach to life, doing things that you want to do, and being happy about what you're doing. If something is awful, think how to make it better and never feel defeated and give up, because thinking positively can eventually turn things around.

JERRY HALL, B. 1956

Winter is on my head,
but eternal spring
is in my heart.

VICTOR HUGO (1802 - 1885)

...cheerfulness keeps up a kind
of daylight in the mind,
and fills it with a steady
and perpetual serenity.

JOSEPH ADDISON (1672 - 1719)

Pessimism leads to weakness,
optimism to power.

AUTHOR UNKNOWN

You are never too old to set another goal
or to dream a new dream.

LES BROWN

Let go the sad times, hold on to
the glad times, the picnics and parties
and fun, the tingle and glow
of a walk in the snow, the lazy days
sprawled in the sun.

PAMELA DUGDALE

One's life has value so long
as one attributes value to the life
of others, by means of love,
friendship, indignation
and compassion.

SIMONE DE BEAUVOIR (1908 - 1986)

*We are all
in the gutter,
but some of us
are looking
at the stars.*

OSCAR WILDE (1854 - 1900)

*I am an indestructible
fortress,
I am an unassailable
rock,
I am a precious
jewel.*

IRISH SAYING

The more you praise and celebrate your life, the more there is in life to celebrate.

OPRAH WINFREY, B. 1954

Some people see things as they are
and say why. I dream things that never were
and say why not.

ROBERT F. KENNEDY JR. (1925 - 1968)

Your attitude is like a box of crayons that color
your world. Constantly color your picture gray,
and your picture will always be bleak.
Try adding some bright colors to the picture
by including humor, and your picture begins to
lighten up.

ALLEN KLEIN (1931 - 2009)

Perpetual optimism

In the long run, the pessimist may be proved to be right, but the optimist has a better time on the trip.

DANIEL L. REARDON

force multiplier.

COLIN L. POWELL, B. 1937

Turn your face to the sun and the shadows fall behind you.

MAORI PROVERB

Avoid negative people; they take away your dreams.

STUART & LINDA MACFARLANE

*Every day is a renewal,
every morning
the daily miracle.
This joy you feel is life.*

GERTRUDE STEIN (1874 - 1946)

You can have anything you want
if you want it desperately enough.
You must want it with an
exuberance that erupts through
the skin and joins the energy that
created the world.

SHEILA GRAHAM

You can't turn back
the clock.
But you can
wind it up again.

BONNIE PRUDDEN

Life is short and in the brief time we are here we should be the best, the boldest and the brightest we can be.

SHAUN MCILWRATH

A strong positive mental attitude will create more miracles than any wonder drug.

PATRICIA NEAL (1926 - 2010)

The most wonderful thing in the world is to be who you are.

LEONTYNE PRICE, B. 1927

Twenty years from now you will be more disappointed by the things that you didn't do than the ones you did do. So throw off the bowlines. Sail away from safe harbour. Catch the trade winds in your sails. Explore. Dream. Discover.

MARK TWAIN (1835 - 1910)

My house
is burned down,
but I can see
the sky.

SALLY REED

Don't judge each day
by the harvest you reap,
but by the seeds that you plant.

ROBERT LOUIS STEVENSON (1850 - 1894)

We all carry it within us:
supreme strength, the fullness of wisdom,
unquenchable joy. It is never
thwarted, and cannot be destroyed.

HUSTON SMITH

*L*ife is 10%
*what happens to us
and 90%
how we react to it.*

CHARLES SWINDOLL, B. 1934

Look to this day! Look to this day! For it is life, the very life of life. In its brief course lie all the varieties and realities of your existence: the bliss of growth, the glory of action, the splendour of beauty. For yesterday is already a dream and tomorrow is only a vision but today, well-lived, makes every yesterday a dream of happiness, and every tomorrow a vision of hope.

Look well, therefore, to this day!

Such is the salutation of the dawn.

SANSKRIT

Believe you can and you're halfway there.

THEODORE ROOSEVELT (1858 - 1919)

Join the whole of creation of animate things in a deep, heartfelt joy that you are alive; that you see the sun, that you are in this glorious earth which nature has made so beautiful and which is yours to conquer and enjoy.

DR. WILLIAM OSLER (1849 - 1919)

All shall be well, and all shall be well and all manner of things shall be well.

JULIAN OF NORWICH (1342 - 1416)

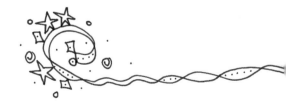

*Every day
it's nice to stop
and say,
"Wait a minute!
I am so lucky!
This is great!"*

KATE HUDSON, B. 1979

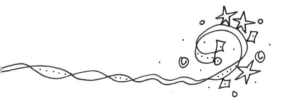

*K*eep your face to the sunshine and you cannot see the shadow.

HELEN KELLER
(BORN BOTH DEAF AND BLIND) (1880 - 1968)

Today I live in the quiet, joyous expectation of good.

ERNEST HOLMES (1887 - 1960)

Believing in negative thoughts is the single greatest obstruction to success.

CHARLES F. GLASSMAN

Put a grain of boldness into everything you do.

BALTASAR GRACIAN (1601 - 1658)

The dark forest, destroyed by summer fires, will grow again. New trees and wildflowers will flourish in sunlight that was never there before.

SUSAN SQUELLATI FLORENCE

If you are hopeful and determined, you will always find some measure of success. Winning the gold medal does not matter. You will have tried your best.

THE DALAI LAMA, B. 1935

Whatever you are,
make sure
you are a good one.

ABRAHAM LINCOLN (1809 - 1865)

I have smelt all the aromas

there are in the fragrant kitchen

they call Earth;

and what we can enjoy in this life,

I surely have enjoyed just like a lord!

HEINRICH HEINE (1797 - 1856)

Each day the first da

Positive thinking is powerful thinking.

GERMANY KENT, B. 1975

ach day a life.

DAG HAMMARSKJÖLD (1905 - 1961)

Small opportunities are often the beginning
of great enterprises.

DEMOSTHENES (384 B.C. - 322 B.C.)

If opportunity doesn't knock,
build a door.

MILTON BERLE (1908 - 2002)

There is not a short life or a long life. There is only the life that you have, and the life you have is the life you are given, the life you work with. It has its own shape, describes its own arc, and is perfect.

GREEK PROVERB

A great attitude becomes a great day which becomes a great month which becomes a great year which becomes a great life.

MANDY HALE

Never measure the height of a mountain, until you have reached the top. Then you will see how low it was.

DAG HAMMARSKJÖLD (1905 - 1961)

*Throw your heart
out in front
of you
And run ahead
to catch it.*

ARAB PROVERB

I thought I'd take style to its limit…
My philosophy is a belief in magic, good luck,
self-confidence and pride.

GRACE JONES, B. 1952

Don't look at your feet to see if you are doing
it right. Just dance.

ANNE LAMOTT, B. 1954

After rain comes fair weather.

JAMES HOWELL (1594 - 1666)

When you have only
two pennies
left in the world,
buy a loaf of bread
with one,
and a lily with the other.

CHINESE PROVERB

Let us rise up and be thankful, for if we didn't learn a lot today at least we learned a little, and if we didn't learn a little, at least we didn't get sick, and if we got sick, at least we didn't die; so let us all be thankful!

GAUTAMA BUDDHA (c.563 B.C. - 483 B.C.)

Enthusiasm moves the world.

J. BALFOUR

To love what you do
and feel that it matters –
how could anything
be more fun?

KATHARINE GRAHAM (1917 - 2001)

*The mind is a powerful thing.
From the tip of my toes
to the last hair on my head,
I had complete confidence.*

JOE LOUIS (1914 - 1981)

A journey of a thousand miles begins with one step.

LAO TZU (604 B.C. - 531 B.C.)

I never saw a pessimistic general win a battle.

DWIGHT D. EISENHOWER (1890 - 1969)

Keep your thoughts positive
because your thoughts
become your words.
Keep your words positive
because your words
become your behaviour.
Keep your behaviour positive
because your behaviour
becomes your habits.
Keep your habits positive
because your habits
become your values.
Keep your values positive
because your values
become your destiny.

MAHATMA GANDHI (1869 - 1948)

*There are only
two ways to live your life.
One is as though
nothing is a miracle.
The other is as though
everything is a miracle.*

ALBERT EINSTEIN (1879 - 1955)

*To live is so startling
it leaves little time
for anything else.*

EMILY DICKINSON (1830 - 1886)

*N*o monument.
No city.
No nation.
Nothing worthwhile
has ever been built
without hope.

STUART & LINDA MACFARLANE

I don't think
of all the misery,
but of the beauty
that still remains.

ANNE FRANK (1929 - 1945)

I am where I am because I believe in all possibilities.

WHOOPI GOLDBERG, B. 1955